The Dale Penin Path

by

Phil Bradfield and Andrew Denyer

A guided walk with on-line resources

www.Walking-Guides.co.uk

First published by Phil Bradfield and Andrew Denyer 2012

ISBN 978-0-9572947-0-7

Printed by Grosvenor Group (Print Services) Ltd.
www.grosvenorgroupltd.co.uk

The Pembrokeshire Coast National Park

The Dale Peninsula

Introduction

Phil Bradfield

I first came to Dale in 1980, as a recently qualified biology teacher accompanying students on their A-Level field trips to Dale Fort Field Centre. I soon fell in love with the area, and have visited Pembrokeshire many times since, in my former job as a teacher and on family holidays.

One of the attractions of Dale is the fact that it is a peninsula. You can walk around the 6 miles (10 km) or so of the coastal path in a few hours, or adopt a more leisurely pace and spread the walk over a day. Because it's a circular walk, at the end you aren't stuck for a lift back!

The location of Dale has endowed it with more than its fair share of archaeological and historical remains. It is situated on the west coast of Wales, where the shape of the peninsula, jutting out to face the entrance to the great natural port of Milford Haven, has brought about the construction of a number of encampments and military constructions. These span human history, from Bronze-age settlements through to Victorian forts and a Second World War airfield.

As a biologist, but with interests in geology, history and archaeology and a liking for walks, to me Dale has always seemed perfect. It's got everything – natural history, birds, beaches and rocky shores, geology, abandoned military installations and archaeological sites. Its location in a rural part of Wales is well away from major cities, so that many sites of interest are in a good state of preservation. Add to that a mild and pleasant climate for most of the year, and you have the ideal place for a walk.

A few years ago I through my work with the Open University, I met Andrew Denyer. We collaborated on a project with the OU, producing materials for a 'podcast' guide to a coastal walk in Devon. I mentioned Dale to Andrew at the time, saying that it would be an excellent place for another guided walk. At last it's come to fruition!

We are indebted to the late John Barrett for his excellent little guide 'The Dale Peninsula'. It provided us with much of the information and inspiration for putting together this booklet. However, Barrett's guide was written in 1966 and updated in 1980, so we thought it was high time to review the coast walk and see what the route has to offer today. In addition we wanted to introduce modern technology to our guide, in the form of accompanying resources on the website.

For a fit person, the walk is not strenuous. It follows the coastal path for most of the way. You should wear suitable clothing and walking shoes or boots, and take a supply of water and food with you to last several hours. There is nowhere to buy food or drink along the way, until you return to Dale village at the end of the walk.

The Ordnance Survey map to use is the Explorer Map (1:25 000) South Pembrokeshire Sheet OL36.

The website

Andrew Denyer

To complement this guide, our website www.Walking-Guides.co.uk provides some useful resources to help you plan and enjoy your visit to the Dale Peninsula.

Phil and I have recorded a number of short conversations we had when he showed me round the route. These are available for download from the website to your mp3 player, and can be listened to along the walk, or at home before you go.

The website contains further photographs, information and links to other websites.

Dale Point, with the entrance to Dale Roads beyond the Point

The Walk

Starting the walk

You enter Dale along the B4327, following the one-way system into the village. There is a 'pay and display' car park near the road, close to the sea front. After you have left the car, continue along the road towards the houses. Head for the Griffin Inn, about 200 metres from the car park.

Stop 1 The Griffin Inn (0 m)

The Griffin Inn

Some sources say that in the 18th century there were as many as 18 inns and alehouses in Dale! The Griffin is the last one remaining. It was originally called the Three Horseshoes, and became the Griffin in 1824. Just along from the pub you will see a sign for the Field Studies Centre. This is the beginning of the road to Dale Fort, the start of your circular walk.

Road to Dale Fort

On your left past the yacht club are four houses, alongside what was once Dale Quay. These buildings date from the 18th and 19th centuries. They are all now private residences, but their original uses were very different. Look out for the names on some of the houses, which indicate something of their history.

The first house was once a general store called Polly Morgan's. The Morgans were sister and brother, who kept the shop up until their deaths in 1938 and 1941. Their store sold all manner of stock, amassed over the years. After their deaths it became a ruin, infested by rats, until it was rebuilt and converted into a house.

The second house on Dale Quay was once the Tabernacle Congregational Chapel, built in 1838 and converted into a house in 1976.

The third house was Artie's Cottage, once occupied by Artie Reynolds, a local character. The last house along the quay was an inn called the Brig. This building dates from 1750. The inn changed names several times. Originally it was called the Ship, and then the Royal William, becoming the Brig in 1893.

The houses along Dale Quay

Continue up the road towards Dale Fort. The next stop follows a walk of about 1000 metres, when you reach the top of the hill and emerge from the trees.

As you make your way up the hill there are some things to look out for.

At the foot of the hill there is a wood to your right, which borders the southern edge of the village. It is called Blue Anchor Wood, named after another long-gone pub. The wood continues to the left of the road as Point Wood, which runs along the north-east coast of the Dale peninsula.

A satellite view shows that woods of Dale are all located on the north and east sides of the peninsula (see the map on page 3). Few trees grow to the south or west, except in sheltered valleys. This is due to the prevailing winds, which are from the south-west.

With its exposed position on the coast, Dale can be a very windy place. These winds, together with salt spray, stunt the growth of trees. Later on along the walk look out for trees that have a peculiar shape, appearing to bend away from the wind. This is caused by a phenomenon called 'wind pruning'. Wind prevents the buds from growing on the windward side, causing more growth to take place on the sheltered (leeward) side, so the trees lean away from the wind.

On the right-hand side of the road across from the houses are the ruins of some cottages. These were still inhabited up until the 1950s.

Construction of the military road to Dale Fort began in 1853. Either side of the road near the top of the hill, look out for the old galvanised iron fence posts with their decorative caps, in amongst the modern barbed wire. They are over 160 years old.

Victorian fence post

Stop 2: (1000 m) Top of the road past the trees, overlooking Dale Roads

The bay between the Dale peninsula and the part of Pembrokeshire to the north is called Dale Roads. From this vantage point you get a wonderful view of the bay, usually full of small sailing boats and other craft. Take some time to admire the scene.

The circular walk follows the Pembrokeshire Coast Path through a gate on the right, about 50 metres further on. Before continuing this way, you will want to go down the road to look at the fort.

Dale Roads

Stop 3: (200 m) Inner gateway to Dale Fort

The fort is now a field centre run by the Field Studies Council. It is private property, but it is fine for you to go through the outer entrance and down to the main gateway. Notice the defensive ditch just outside the walls of the fort. The bridge over this ditch was once a drawbridge. Just inside the gateway is a public information board detailing the history of the fort.

Entrance to Dale Fort

For groups of walkers, it is possible to phone the centre in advance to arrange a visit – if a member of staff is available they will be happy to show you round.

You can also go on a 'virtual tour' of the fort (see www.Walking-Guides.co.uk for a link to the fort's website).

This Victorian fort was completed in 1856 as a part of a system of twelve fortifications and barracks sited around the entrance to Milford Haven. These constructions were principally designed to deter the forces of Napoleon III of France from attacking the Haven and the naval dockyard at Pembroke Dock. Charles Louis Napoleon had been president of France since 1848, and in 1851 he was given an overwhelming mandate from the French electorate to dissolve the French Second Republic and become emperor. His fighting talk panicked the British government into improving coastal defences of southern England and Wales against invasion. As we now know, these were never used, except as a deterrent. They had only minor uses in later wars.

In the early years the fort was manned by a garrison of sixty soldiers, along with some of their wives and families. By 1861 it mounted seven large (68-pound) smooth bore muzzle-loading cannons facing out to sea. There were also two smaller (32-pound) cannons pointing inland, to defend against the building being outflanked from the landward side.

Outer defensive wall of the gun parapet

However, even by the time these cannons were installed, rapid developments in artillery and warship construction had made smooth bore, muzzle-loaders obsolete, so the outer cannons were converted to rifled (but still muzzle-loading) guns. These were more accurate, and able to fire solid shot that could penetrate the armour of the new 'ironclad' warships.

By the 1870s, with the threat of invasion long gone, the garrison had been reduced to eleven soldiers and their families.

In the 1890s, further improvements in warship technology meant that the guns of the fort were again inadequate. This led to an experiment with an unusual American invention, the Zalinski pneumatic dynamite gun. This was a weapon with a barrel 38 cm in diameter and 17 metres in length, which could fire a dynamite-filled shell weighing half a ton a distance of 3 km.

The propulsive force to fire the shell was compressed air, stored in huge underground tanks. Compressed air had to be used because conventional explosive charges would cause the dynamite to explode in the gun barrel.

Although this strange weapon was reliable and accurate, it was soon to be superseded by the invention of stable explosives that allowed an explosive shell to be fired from conventional guns. The Zalinski gun was only in place for a few years before being scrapped.

The Zalinski gun – details from the information board at the fort

You can see photos of the gun on the fort information board. The remains of its circular gun emplacement are still in situ at the top of the fort above the laboratories.

In 1902 the fort was sold to Lieutenant Colonel A. Owen-Evans, who began converting it into a private residence for himself and his family. During the First World War Colonel Owen-Evans allowed it to be used as a military hospital. It was also a signal station and formed one end of the Haven's boom defence.

After the Colonel's death in 1925, the fort was sold to a Miss M.A Bland, later Mrs Lee-Roberts.

Mrs Lee-Roberts made improvements to the property, such as introducing an electricity supply and building the glasshouse conservatories you can see just beyond the main doorway.

When Mrs Lee-Roberts moved out of the fort in 1942, it was taken over by the Admiralty and put to various wartime uses. These included watching for sea mines, and overseeing the 'de-gaussing' of ships in Milford Haven.

Enemy aircraft dropped magnetic mines that sat on the sea bottom until they were set off by the magnetic field of a passing ship. De-gaussing involved altering a ship's magnetic field using electric coils, so that it would not cause a mine to detonate.

After the war, Dale Fort was established as a field centre in 1947. It is now one of seventeen centres run by the Field Studies Council. It puts on courses in biology, geography and ecology, catering for students from primary school through to university level. It also organises courses for individuals and families covering a range of subjects, such as natural history, art, photography, history and archaeology.

Now walk back the way you came, and find the gate on the left with a signpost for the Coast Path.

Stop 4: (150 m) Gate with signpost indicating the Coast Path

Dale Point is a coastal promontory ending in steep cliffs. Geographical locations like this are relatively easy places to organise defences against an attacker, and the Victorian fort was not the first fortification built here. Just after you pass through the gate you can see earth mounds that are the remains of the outer rampart and ditch of an Iron Age fort. The gap in the mound marks the position of the entrance to the fort.

Defensive bank of the Iron Age fort

A small community or tribe probably lived on the promontory side, protected by the rampart and ditch, while they farmed the land outside the bank.

The Iron Age fort has been excavated a number of times between the 1960s and 2007. The archaeological evidence shows that the earliest habitation was in the early Bronze Age, about 4000 years ago.

The walls of the defensive bank were developed and strengthened with large stones later in the Iron Age, around 600 BC.

Continue along the coast path and down the hill until you reach an inlet called Castlebeach.

Stop 5: (450 m) Wooden bridge at the top of Castlebeach

Next to the wooden bridge over the small stream are the ruins of a limekiln. As with most of Pembrokeshire, the soils of the Dale peninsula are acidic, and benefit from treatment with lime to improve the growth of crops.

Limekiln at the top of Castlebeach

Limestone and coal were brought in by sea and placed in layers in the kiln. Using the coal as fuel, the limestone (calcium carbonate) was burnt in the kiln for several days and then allowed to cool. The whole process took about a week. The end product was quicklime (calcium oxide), which was used to neutralise the acid soil.

The last time this kiln was used was at the beginning of the 20th century. The coming of the railways and industrial scale production of lime made local lime-burning uneconomic.

Walk down to the beach. Castlebeach always seems to have more than its fair share of accumulated rubbish from ships – plastic containers, polystyrene, driftwood, nets, bottles and the like. It is a peculiarity of the tides and ocean currents that cause so much pollutant debris to end up stranded on this beach.

Debris stranded on Castlebeach

The rock making up the cliffs either side of the beach is known as Old Red Sandstone (ORS). ORS is a sedimentary rock. The sediments that formed ORS were produced in hot, dry desert conditions and deposited in coastal plains and river deltas during the early Devonian period, about 400 million years ago.

The red colour of ORS is due to iron oxide coating the quartz crystals of the rock. This oxide is similar in composition to rust, and dissolves in seawater. If you compare the cliffs with the sand on the beach, you can see what happens when the rock is eroded and weathered by the sea – the iron oxide dissolves and the quartz sand grains left behind are the more familiar sandy colour. This tells us that unlike most sedimentary rocks, ORS was not laid down in a marine environment.

Geologists call the layers of sedimentary rock 'strata'. When they were first deposited they would have been horizontal, but during the Earth's history they have been folded by the movement of tectonic plates in the Earth's crust. So a section through the rocks shows the strata lying at an angle. This is called the angle of dip. The ORS strata of the cliffs dip to the south at about 70°. This is easier to see if you take a look back at the cliffs of Dale Point.

The rocks of the cliff walls are covered by living organisms. These form coloured horizontal bands. At the top of the cliff, there is a green band made up of land plants such as grasses and sea pinks. These plants can only survive above the splash zone, where they are not often subjected to splashing by salt water. Below this is a band containing pale grey and orange lichens. These organisms can survive splashing with the salt water, but not prolonged immersion in the sea. Next is a black band, made up of a lichen species that is better at surviving longer periods under water.

Bands (zones) of organisms on the old red sandstone rocks at Castlebeach

Below the black lichen we start to see the truly marine organisms.

On Castlebeach there is a thin layer of yellow-brown seaweeds, mainly on the sheltered sides of the rocks, and below this a grey layer of barnacles and limpets.

Biologists call the development of these bands of organisms 'zonation'. Further up the cliff, the organisms will spend less time immersed in seawater as the tides go in and out. Each species is adapted to a different period of immersion, and so they form bands. If you look back across the bay towards Dale Point again, you can see the zonation on the rocks there.

Walk back to the bridge and continue along the coast path. The walk takes you uphill and through a couple of gates.

Stop 6: (570 m) Irrigation pond next to the path

Irrigation pond

The pond to the right of the path was made by damming a small stream. Water is pumped up to the farmland above and used for irrigating crops. Notice the luxuriant growth of plants and trees to the left of the path where the stream runs down the cliff. You are still on the sheltered, western side of the peninsula, where growth of trees is possible. In the distance you can see a tall navigation tower, which is your next stop. Walk up and over the top of the hill, through a gate.

Stop 7: (330 m) The navigation tower

The navigation tower

This navigation tower was built in 1970, and is over 58 metres high. The deep-water channel into Milford Haven is very narrow, so tankers, ferries and other large vessels have to be sure of their approach to the Haven.

View of Dale Point from the navigation tower

From the open sea, ships first follow a north-easterly route, followed by a dog-leg change of direction to the east.

There is another set of three navigation towers with lights at West Blockhouse Point (Stop 10 on your walk). Ships out at sea can line up this tower with the central one at West Blockhouse, in order to judge the correct angle of approach to the Haven.

Looking back towards Castlebeach Bay you can see how dense the trees are in this sheltered part of the peninsula. Across the bay you get a good view of Dale Fort. Notice the protective ditch reaching down to the sea on the landward side, and the gun parapet facing out to sea. The parapet is surrounded by walls made of limestone 1.4 metres thick, capped with granite (see the photo on page 9).

Stop 8: (320 m) Cattle grid

From the highest vantage point close to the cattle grid, look inland across the peninsula. You will see that the landscape is flat. This level surface was cut by ancient seas, and is called a wave-cut platform.

About 17 million years ago the average surface temperature of the Earth was warmer, the polar ice caps had melted and the sea level was about 60 metres higher than it is today. The sea eroded the land surface to form this flat topography, which is known as a wave-cut platform. The same process is happening today, at modern-day sea levels. You can see this later along the walk, at Great Castle Bay (Stop 16).

You now have a fairly long walk to your next stop, Watwick Bay. Continue along the Coast Path for about 500 metres, and then take the side path down to the bay.

The path down is steep in places, so if you prefer, you can leave out this section of the walk and continue along the Coast Path to Stop 10.

Stop 9: (880 m) Watwick Bay

Watwick Bay from the south

The suffix '-wick' is Norse for a bay.

Notice the dense growth of shrubs, ferns and other plants either side of the path down to the bay. This area is still sheltered from the prevailing south-westerly winds, and plant growth is encouraged by the still, humid conditions. A small stream runs down the bottom of the valley. Around the outfall of the stream on the beach, marsh plants such as irises are able to grow.

The cliffs on either side of the bay are again made of Old Red Sandstone. Look at the strata of the rocks – on the north side they slope (dip) to the south, as at Dale Fort. But on the south side they dip to the north. In other words, on either side of the bay the angle of dip is towards the middle.

Steeply dipping rock strata

The rocks have been folded downwards into a trough-like shape, which geologists call a syncline. The axis of the fold runs down the centre of the bay.

In fact the whole of the Dale peninsula is a syncline, with its axis running across the peninsula, from to here at Watwick Bay in the east to Kete in the west (Stop 14).

Make your way back up the path to re-join the Coast Path at the top of the valley. The walk continues along towards West Blockhouse Point on the next promontory.

Stop 10: (810 m) The stone bench at West Blockhouse Point

Stone bench at West Blockhouse Point

The bench is dedicated to Brigadier C.T.W. Gough O.B.E, who served at the fort from 1931-35.

There have been fortifications at West Blockhouse Point from at least the times of Henry VIII, when a fortified round 'artillery tower' stood on this spot. West Blockhouse Fort was constructed on the site of this tower in 1857, as part of the protective fortifications around the entrance to Milford Haven, which include Dale Fort (Stop 3).

Originally, the fort mounted six 68-pounder muzzle-loading cannons, and had a garrison of up to 40 men and an officer. In 1901 it was remodelled, and fitted with four 5-inch breech-loading guns in the main battery, and two 3-pounder quick-firing guns on the roof.

View from above West Blockhouse Fort

Later, in 1904-5, a further battery was built on the land 150 metres above and west of the fort. At first this battery contained two 9.2-inch, and three 6-inch breech-loading guns.

Gun emplacement of the upper battery. The navigation towers are in the background

Over the first half of the 20th century the emplacements and guns were modified from time to time, and they continued in use throughout both World Wars. A searchlight battery was added later, below the fort. The fort was finally closed in 1950.

The final occupation of the fort was by a corporal and six young men, 'enjoying' their National Service.

The fort is now owned by the Landmark Trust, and rented out as holiday accommodation. It is not open to the general public.

The gun emplacements above the fort are still in position. There is easy access to these, but you should first ask permission from the Landmark Trust.

Upper battery – ammunition storage buildings

The three navigation towers to the right of the fort are between 9 and 14 metres in height. They are equipped with marker boards, lights, radar beacons and a foghorn. They are known as 'leading light' beacons, used for position fixing and indicating a safe passage into Milford Haven.

The Coast Path now takes a short detour inland before returning to the coast. Follow the signposts, which take you round Mill Bay.

Stop 11: (1000 m) Mill Bay

The name 'Mill Bay' is marked on maps from as long ago as 1595, although there is no mill here now.

The remains of a masonry wall at the top of the beach might possibly be the remains of a mill. Nearby are the few remaining parts of a vessel that was wrecked here in 1964. Luckily it was only a ship being towed to Swansea for scrap.

Mill Bay was the site of an important event in English history. On Sunday 7th August 1485, Henry Tudor (Henry VII), landed in the bay from his exile in Brittany. He marched inland to England, on the way collecting an army of 5000 men. On 22nd August he defeated Richard III at the Battle of Bosworth Field, bringing the 'Wars of the Roses' to an end, and starting the Tudor dynasty.

Mill Bay

As at Castlebeach, a small stream runs along the bottom of the valley. These streams are far too small to have cut through the cliffs to form the valley – a much greater force was needed. This was supplied by melting ice after the last 'ice age'.

This last glacial period in the Earth's recent geological history lasted from about 110 000 to 10 000 years ago, with the maximum extent of glaciation occurring about 18 000 years before the present day. The southern limit of glaciers in this part of Britain was at about the latitude of the Dale peninsula. Since then the climate has warmed, and the ice sheets have retreated (although technically we are still in an 'ice age' since ice sheets still cover much of the poles).

At the maximum stage of glaciation, sea level fell by about 75 metres (compare this with the elevated sea levels discussed at Stop 8). Then the ice melted and the glaciers retreated northwards. Vast volumes of melt water flowed down the valleys of the time, making them deeper and wider – much more so than could have been formed by the small streams existing today.

Continue up the hill to the buildings on St Ann's Head. Beside the path above the bay is an information board describing the landing of Henry Tudor. The Coast Path continues past a derelict walled garden and up across a field towards the lighthouse on St. Ann's Head.

Information board about the landing of Henry Tudor

Path to St. Ann's Head by walled garden

Stop 12: (730 m) Halfway between the two lighthouses on St. Ann's Head

St. Ann's Head was once the location of a chapel built by Henry Tudor to mark his landing place. The chapel did not survive for long, and is known to have been derelict by 1600. It is thought that a primitive lighthouse consisting of a coal-fired brazier probably existed around this time.

Trinity House oversaw the building of two new lighthouses on the Head in 1714, consisting of a taller 'high light' and a 'low light' 200 metres away. In 1841 the 'low light' was rebuilt, under the supervision of John Knott, the senior lighthouse keeper with Trinity House. This is the modern functioning lighthouse, the last remaining shore-based lighthouse in Pembrokeshire. It was converted to mains electricity in 1958, and automated in 1998.

The footpath across the field takes you quite close to the new lighthouse buildings, although there is no public access to the site. The Coast Path continues along the metalled road past the old 'high light'.

The 'high light' was decommissioned in 1910. Just before the Second World War its lantern was removed and a concrete observation room added on the top of the structure, after which it became the Milford Haven Fire Command Headquarters. During the war it acted as the Royal Navy's Port War Signal Station, with the role of identifying any warships or submarines approaching Milford Haven. After the war it became the Coastguard Station. It is now used for holiday accommodation.

The round building halfway between the old and new lighthouses houses the foghorn. About 100 metres behind it is a helicopter-landing pad. It is used by Trinity House to service offshore lighthouses. Beyond the helipad, near the cliff edge, is a small square building that housed the original foghorn.

The old 'high light' lighthouse

The new 'low light' lighthouse and keepers' cottages

If you have a head for heights, you can walk along the path close to the old foghorn house and look out towards a cut into the Headland called Cobbler's Hole. The rocks on the far side are deformed into down-folds (synclines) and up-folds (anticlines). This folding was caused by movement of plates in the Earth's crust, causing them to push against each other. In places you can see faults in the rocks – the folding has caused a fracture in the strata so that the beds on one side of the fault are displaced relative to the other.

On top of the Old Red Sandstone are layers of younger rocks – limestone, millstone grit and coal measures from the Carboniferous period (354 to 290 million years ago).

Folded rocks at Cobbler's Hole

The Coast Path continues along the road towards a boundary wall that cuts off the headland.

During the First World War St. Ann's Head had a similar role to that in WW2, with an observation post looking out to sea. All evidence of WW1 artefacts has disappeared, except for holes cut into the boundary wall at intervals. These are rifle loopholes that would have been used to defend the Trinity House land from attack from the landward side. During the Second World War the defences were augmented by barbed wire and a minefield outside the boundary wall.

Boundary wall with loophole

Follow the Coast Path through the entrance in the boundary wall and turn left through the gate. The steep-sided inlet to the left is called the Vomit, named after the plumes of sea-spray that rush upwards from the inlet during westerly gales. The path follows close to the cliff edge for some distance. Take care along this stretch. Follow the signposted route, and make sure you stop when observing your surroundings.

Looking back towards St Ann's Head

You are now walking up the west coast of the peninsula. The vegetation here is different from that on the sheltered east coast. As we discussed earlier, there are no woods on this part of the coast, just short turf with a profusion of different low-growing species of flowering plants, and the occasional stunted wind-pruned tree.

A profusion of flowers beside the path in spring

The ornithologists among you will have plenty of species to look out for. As well as gulls, fulmars and jackdaws, look out for less common birds such as choughs, storm petrels, buzzards and wheatears that make an appearance around St. Ann's Head. Porpoises and dolphins are also regularly spotted off the Head.

The next stop is some distance ahead, but there is plenty of natural history for you to enjoy as you walk along the cliff path.

Stop 13: (700 m) Vomit Point: a view of the islands

Vomit Point is the next headland around the coast from St. Ann's Head.

On a clear day you can get a good view of the nearby islands from the tip of the Point, or from any of the headlands along this west coast of the peninsula.

The two largest islands are Skokholm and Skomer, both managed by the Wildlife Trust of South and West Wales.

As you look out to sea the island to the left (i.e. furthest south) and about 5 kilometres distant is Skokholm. It is about a kilometre in length and half a kilometre in width. A Site of Special Scientific Interest (SSSI), it is home to 45 000 pairs of Manx shearwaters and 2000 pairs of puffins, as well as several other bird species, including guillemots, razorbills, storm petrels and choughs. Landing on the island is not permitted, apart from pre-arranged trips from Martin's Haven on the mainland (see www.Walking-Guides.co.uk for a link to the Wildlife Trust's website).

The island to the right, about 4 kilometres north of Skokholm, is Skomer. It is a little larger than Skokholm, with an area of about 3 square kilometres. Despite this relatively small size, it is one of the most important wildlife locations in Europe. As well as being an SSSI, a Special Protection Area, and a National Nature Reserve, it is surrounded by a Marine Nature Reserve.

Skomer has the world's largest breeding colony of Manx shearwaters (150 000 pairs), as well as 6000 pairs of puffins, and large colonies of guillemots, lesser black-backed gulls, kittiwakes, razorbills, fulmars and other species.

Skomer is home to a unique mammal species, the Skomer vole, which is preyed upon by short-eared owls. Around the coast of the island grey seals are usually seen basking on the rocks. Much of the island is also a designated Ancient Monument, with remains such as a Neolithic stone circle.

Boats sail to Skomer from Martin's Haven, from April through to October. One of the best times to visit is April or May, when the island is covered by a profusion of bluebells and red campions.

Skomer in spring

Continue your walk along the Coast Path, which follows the cliff edge around a bay called Frenchman's Bay.

Stop 14: (810 m) Gate entering National Trust land (Kete)

Entrance to Kete

As you walk along the next kilometre or so of Coast Path, it is difficult to believe that the fields to your right once contained over a hundred huts and other buildings, with many hundreds of working Service personnel. Today the only evidence of all this activity consists of lumps of brick and concrete beside the path, and some concrete roadways inland. Near the road crossing the peninsula is a single remaining hut, now used as a farm building, and a couple of houses that were built as officers' quarters.

The first military station here was RAF Kete, which opened early during World War Two. Kete was not an airfield, but a Chain Home Low (CHL) radar station, with the role of tracking low-flying enemy aircraft, and training radar technicians and Fighter Direction Officers.

One remaining Kete building – a radar hut, now a farm building

In 1943 the control of Kete passed to the Royal Navy, and it became HMS Goldcrest 2 (Goldcrest 1 was Dale airfield – see Stop 17a). In 1948 it was commissioned as HMS Harrier, a Royal Navy Fighter Direction School and School of Meteorology. At its peak, the huts of HMS Harrier provided accommodation, classrooms and offices for over 1500 sailors, 'wrens' and civilians employees.

HMS Harrier closed in 1960. Afterwards the derelict buildings were cleared (apparently by bulldozing them, judging by the heaps of building material piled up in banks around the site!) The freehold of Kete was passed to the National Trust in 1967.

Rubble from the Kete buildings

You will have a longish walk of over a kilometre before the next stop, at the end of the National Trust land. All along this stretch you can see the bulldozed remains from Kete buildings, now covered by grasses and other flowering plants.

Stop 15: (1210 m) Long Point

Ponies on Kete land near Long Point

You have just walked around Welshman's Bay, which ends at a promontory called Long Point.

Along this stretch the view inland shows the ancient wave-cut platform discussed at Stop 8.

In places along this stretch, the exposed rocks of the cliff show evidence of the last glaciation, in the form of a gravelly, stony deposit on the top of the bedrock. This material was carried along by the ice and deposited after the glaciers retreated. Evidence of the effects of glaciation is also revealed by the presence of 'erratics', which are boulders made of rock not found in this part of the country today. They were carried long distances by the ice, sometimes for hundreds of kilometres. The glaciers that covered this region 15-20 000 years ago came down the Irish Sea from Scotland and the Lake District, carrying with them pieces of rock from these areas.

Being on the windward side of the peninsula doesn't just affect the growth of land plants along the coast. The exposure to the wind and waves also influences the distribution of organisms on the rocky shores. On an exposed shore plants and animals of the intertidal zone extend much further up the shore – the vertical distance from the seaweeds on the lower shore to the lichens in the splash zone can be tens of metres, whereas on a sheltered shore on the east of the peninsula it may be only a few metres.

About 500 metres further on you leave the Kete National Trust property. The path carries on around Castle Bay.

Stop 16: (1330 m) Great Castle Head

Great Castle Head is the site of another Iron Age fort, dating from the early to mid first millennium BC. From the path, two defensive banks and ditches can be seen. These would have offered protection from the landward side. As with the Iron Age fort at Dale Point, the occupants would have lived on the seaward side of the banks and farmed the land outside the defences.

Defensive banks of Great Castle Head Iron Age Fort

The fort was excavated by the Dyfed Archaeological Trust in 1999. They reported that although the banks and ditches survive in a reasonable condition, a massive landslip has lowered the land surface on the southern side by many metres, and within the defences only a small portion remains of what would have been the residential area. The excavation found post-holes and pits, and other artefacts such as prehistoric pottery, but no remaining signs of roundhouses. Later Roman and 12th – 13th century pottery was also discovered, suggesting that the fort was remodelled in medieval times.

During World War Two the Head mounted an anti-aircraft and searchlight battery, but no traces of this remain today.

At low tide in Castle Bay a present-day wave-cut platform can be seen. This a modern example produced by the same erosion process that resulted in the flat topography of much of the Dale peninsula (see Stops 8 and 15).

Stop 17: (180 m) West Dale Bay

West Dale Bay

Walk down the path to the beach. Notice the geological material either side of the path. This was deposited after the last glaciation, when the glaciers melted and melt waters carried material down from the sides of the valley. The coarsest material containing pebbles is at the base of the deposits, with the grain size decreasing to fine sands at the top. This is called a 'graded' deposit.

Coarse material was deposited by fast-flowing water. As the valley filled, the flow-rate decreased and finer sands and silts were laid down.

Post-glacial deposits at West Dale Bay

On either side of the bay the rock strata show a different angle of dip, less steep on the south side. In places there are sudden changes in angle.

This valley was formed along a massive system of geological fault lines that extends right up through Milford Haven, under Cardigan Bay and along the top of the Gower Peninsula. When the Earth enters its next warm period and sea levels rise again, the valley will be flooded and the peninsula will become an island.

View of West Dale Bay and Great Castle Head from the north

From the path down to West Dale Bay you can continue the circular walk around the peninsula back to Dale, or alternatively take a short detour off the circular path to visit Dale airfield. For those of you who are interested in Second World War heritage sites, it is well worth the visit.

To see the airfield, continue along the coast path, taking the steps up to the top of the hill. Go through the gate, turn right and walk a short distance to the gated entrance road. The southern perimeter road of the airfield is 200 metres along this road. A path marked on Ordnance Survey maps follows the southern and western perimeter roads, although the airfield itself is private property.

Steps up from West Dale Bay

Coast path above West Dale Bay

Stop 17a: (430 m) Dale airfield

Dale was one of eight airfields that were built in Pembrokeshire during the Second World War. They have the typical pattern of three intersecting runways in a triangle. Dale was a satellite to nearby Talbenny airfield, about 6 kilometres to the north-east. It opened in June 1942 and for a year operated Wellington bombers of No 304 (Polish) squadron. They flew on convoy protection missions as well as bombing raids on ports in occupied France. As well as the dangers experienced on these missions, crews suffered fatalities caused by the difficulties involved in landing the bombers from the sea. One plane crashed into the cliffs as it attempted to land in poor visibility. In Marloes Church there is a roll of honour to the Polish aircrew that served at Dale.

A number of other types of aircraft operated from Dale, including Beauforts, Beaufighters and Mosquitoes.

Dale airfield perimeter road

Dale airfield runway

In September 1943 the airfield was passed to the Royal Navy, and became RNAS Dale (HMS Goldcrest 1) supporting the flight training carried out at Kete (HMS Goldcrest 2). It remained in this role until it closed in 1947.

Dale was an excellent example of a 'dispersed site' airfield. As well as dispersal areas all around the airfield for the aircraft, buildings such as accommodation blocks were sited on farms and other areas well away from the airfield. This offered better protection from enemy action. You can come across derelict wartime RAF buildings all over this part of Pembrokeshire.

Most of the airfield buildings have been demolished, but a skeleton of one hangar still stands, along with several workshops and accommodation buildings on private land to the north-west of the site. One of the huts contains paintings of aircraft and other 'barrack room art', and is a Grade II listed building. It can be visited by arrangement with Coastlands Local History Group (see www.Walking-Guides.co.uk for their web address).

Take the path back down the hill to West Dale Bay (Stop 17). Cross the stile and follow the path along the bottom of the valley towards Dale Castle, visible in the distance.

Dale Valley

Stop 18: (510 m) Dale Castle

Dale castle was originally the site of a Norman castle or tower house. It was built after the English invasion of South Wales, and occupied by the de Vale family from about 1130 to 1300. The male line of the family died out, and subsequent owners rotated through the female line.

Ownership passed to the Walter family of Roch Castle, from whom Lucy Walter, mistress of Charles II and mother of the Duke of Monmouth was descended.

Subsequent owners were the families of the Paynters, Allens and Lloyds. It is now owned by the Lloyd-Philipps family, who sold much of the estate land, including the island of Skokholm.

The modern Castle was rebuilt in 1910, incorporating parts of the medieval castle in the south wing. It is not open to the public.

Dale Castle

Continue along the road to Dale Church.

Stop 19: (120 m) Dale Church

Dale Church

The church is dedicated to St. James. It stands on a Norman site, but was rebuilt in 1761 and underwent substantial repairs in the 1890s. The west tower is thought to date from the 15th Century. It is a simple building, consisting of a nave and chancel. The marble font was presented to the parish by John Allen Esq. of Dale Castle, who met the costs of the 1761 rebuild.

After you have visited the church, walk back towards the Castle and follow the left turn in the road towards the village, a distance of about 880 metres.

The valley between the church and the village is Dale Meadow. During the First World War it was the site of a large camp with huts for 1000 men. Originally it was used for training exercises. Later in the War the camp provided badly needed rest and recuperation facilities for soldiers from that conflict.

The final stage of your walk takes you past Dale Cemetery on your right, and along Blue Anchor Way (see Stop 1).

Dale cemetery

War memorial in Dale cemetery

The houses on the right-hand side of Blue Anchor Way (a row of semis and a terrace) were built as married quarters for Kete, but were barely used for that purpose before Kete closed.

At the end of Blue Anchor Way take the right fork along South Street. Turn left when you get to the sea front. The Griffin Inn is on your left, where you can partake in some well-earned refreshment!

Notes